TRUCKS

SIMON SPOTLIGHT

An imprint of Simon & Schuster Children's Publishing Division

1230 Avenue of the Americas, New York, NY 10020

Text copyright © 2009 by Steven Krensky

Illustrations copyright © 2009 by Ivanke & Lola

All rights reserved, including the right of reproduction in whole or in part in any form.

SIMON SPOTLIGHT and related logo and READY-TO-READ

are registered trademarks of Simon & Schuster, Inc.

Designed by Karin Paprocki

The text of this book was set in Imperfect.

Manufactured in the United States of America

First Aladdin Paperbacks edition May 2009

2 4 6 8 10 9 7 5 3

CIP data for this book is available from the Library of Congress.

ISBN: 978-1-4169-0236-

0817 LAK

TRUCKS

STEPHEN KRENSKY

ILLUSTRATED BY   IVANKE & LOLA

Ready-to-Read

Simon Spotlight

New York   London   Toronto   Sydney   New Delhi

Sun up.
Trucks roll.

Some fast, some slow.

One, two,

three trucks.

Four and more trucks.

Up the tall hill,
over the hump,

down the small hill,

bumpity-bump!

Trucks at work.

Stopping,

dropping.

Pumping.

Dumping.

17

Mixing. ⬉

Fixing.

Big trucks grumble,
big rocks tumble.

Watch trucks filling!

Oops! Look out!
Now trucks spilling.

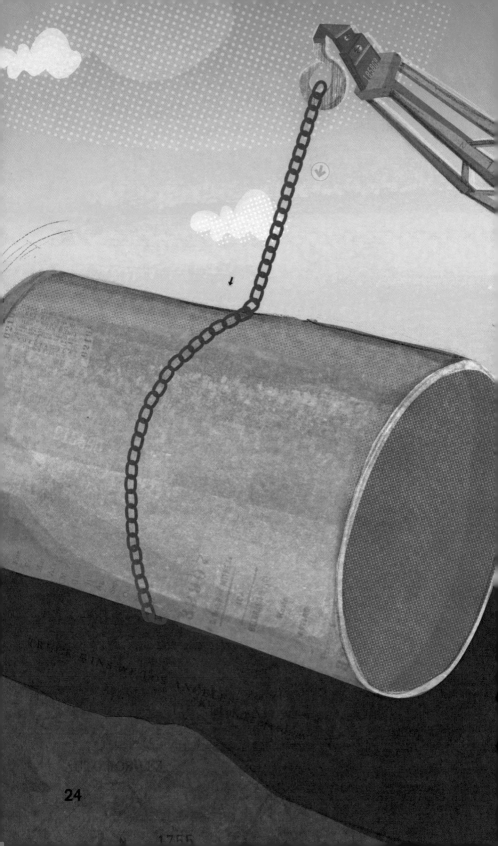

Hours pass.
Shadows grow.

No more sun.
Trucks are done.

One, two, three trucks.

Four and more trucks.

Heading home.
Time to sleep.

Sun up.

Trucks roll.

HONK, HONK!

BEEP-BEEP!

31901062916566